*When did I start to love you?*

To my well-chosen companion on this journey, my lover and my friend.

Library of Congress Catalog Card Number 89-51306
ISBN 0-8423-7982-7
Copyright © 1989 Tyndale House Publishers, Inc.
Text copyright © 1977 by Gloria Gaither
Photography copyright © 1989 by Toshi Otsuki
Printed in the United States of America

1 2 3 4 5 6 7 8 94 93 92 91 90 89

# When did I start to love you?

# GLORIA GAITHER

### PHOTOGRAPHY BY TOSHI OTSUKI

Tyndale House Publishers, Inc.
Wheaton, Illinois

*Does love have a beginning that a meeting's measured by?*

*Does it happen in a moment like white lightning from the sky?*

*Can you tell me its dimensions—just this wide and just this high?*

*When did I start to love you?*

*Tell me just how many dates it takes for love to really start?*

*And just how many kisses will turn "love" into an art?*

*When does the magic moment come to give away your heart?*

*When did I start to love you?*

$W$as the day we talked of Browning the beginning of it all?

Or the time we walked the meadow and the fields of corn so tall

That we felt like naughty children hiding from their mother's call?

When did I start to love you?

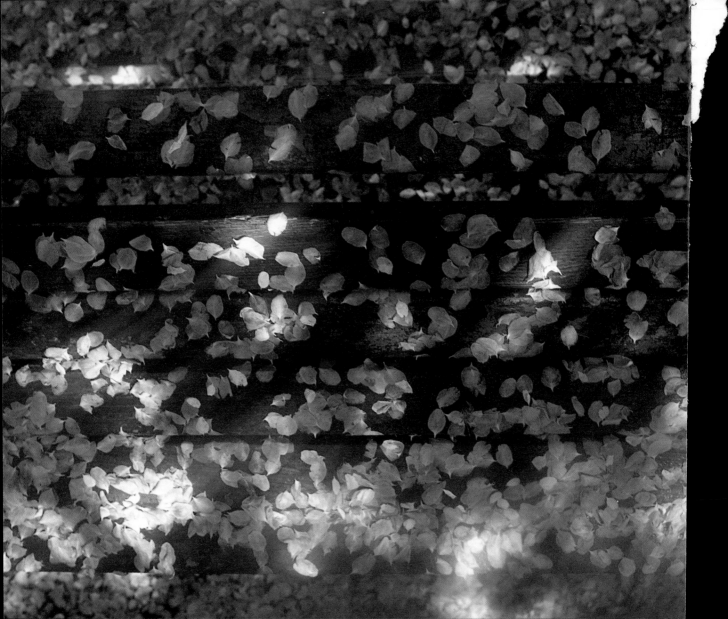

*I* remember just how timidly your first new song you shared—

And by the way you grinned I knew that you were glad you'd dared,

Although my evaluation wasn't worth much, still you **cared**.

When did I start to love you?

Was it when I went to meet you in a gown of snowy white?

Was it when we signed the license and drove off into the night?

Was it when I gave myself to you and felt that it was right?

When did I start to love you?

When I feared you wouldn't love me if you knew how I'd been wrong,

And I spent a week in mis'ry, but you'd known it all along,

And you loved me 'cause you love me, and not because I'm strong!

Was it then I came to love you?

*Was it when we knew for certain 'bout the baby on the way?*

*Did it start the day you told me I looked **pretty—shaped that way?***

*Or did something special happen as we waited that last day....*

*When did I start to love you?*

*Did it happen when we held her in our arms for the first time?*

*Was it later when I nursed her, this creation—yours and mine?*

*And I knew compared to what we held the world's not worth a dime!*

*When did I start to love you?*

*There were nights we stayed and prayed by babies, fevers burning hot,*

*When we really didn't know if they would make it through or not—*

*Then we'd face the dawn's beginning, thanking God for what we've got—*

*When did I start to love you?*

Was it rushing to the clinic with a bone in Amy's throat?

Was it nights you saw me shivering and wrapped me in your coat?

Was it when I cleaned your bureau drawer and found you'd saved my note—

When did I start to love you?

Was it when I saw you showing Benjy how to be a man?

How to sheath his strength in meekness—

How to gently take a stand—

How that only strength of character can salvage this old land?

When did I start to love you?

When you held me close in silence when there were no words for grief—

When the line of empty caskets gaped at all I called "belief"—

When the "amen" was so final. I had you, and dared to leave—

Was it then I came to love you?

*What is the stuff love's made of that can cause the world to glow?*

*Is it that you made the segments that I brought you, well and whole?*

*Was it when I came to recognize the poet in your soul*

    *That I began to love you?*

*It's not of lace and chocolate that valentines are made—*

*All such things are lovely but disintegrate and fade.*

*But love—when once it **grows** to be—is richer far than jade—*

*I only know—I love you!*